SHAKE OFF THE DUST OF DEPRESSION

Exploring Divine Escape Routes

Michael Emmanuel, Ph.D.

To the memory of Dr. Obed, and to Dr. Mrs. Obed, for shaping the foundation of my faith in Christ Jesus.

Contents

Introduction

PAY ATTENTION TO THE WELFARE OF YOUR SOUL

.....Pay attention to the welfare of your innermost being, for from there flows the wellspring of life.
Proverbs 4:23b (TPT)

But the spiritual man has insight into everything, and that bothers and baffles the man of the world, who can't understand him at all.
1 Corinthians 2:15 (LB)

I t is truly alarming and concerning to see the rate at which depression is rising across different age groups, genders, and socioeconomic backgrounds. The persistent feelings of sadness, helplessness, and hopelessness continue to increase. The pandemic has significantly affected working-age adults, with reports of increased stress, anxiety, and depression related to economic uncertainties, remote work challenges, and social isolation.

A rhetorical question, then, is where or who do we go to for help and support? Or is all hope lost? Jeremiah the prophet asked a similar question in Jeremiah 8:22 (AMPC), "Is there no balm in Gilead? Is there no physician there? Why then is not the health of the daughter of my people restored? [Because Zion no longer enjoyed the presence of the Great Physician!]".

I consider depression and associated emotional turmoil one of the most potent enemies of humanity. It did not start with the pandemic, although exacerbated by it, it is man's agelong enemy.

The best of us still struggles with anxiety and feelings of hopelessness and helplessness. But interestingly, look at what God told Cain in Genesis 4:7: "If you do well, will you not be accepted? And if you do not do well, sin lies at the door. And its desire is for you, but you should rule over it.". He said sin crouches at your door; its desire is for you, but you must master it. This is also true for depression. It is crouching at the door of your soul and its desire is for you, but you must master and rule over it. Don't let depression master you but master it. You and I have the sole responsibility to master and bear rule over our emotions. Don't give in to the roller coaster of negative emotions.

Let me remind you that you are not alone in the fight against depression. Rick Warren, the founding pastor of Saddleback Church and author of "The Purpose Driven Life," has spoken openly about his family's struggles with mental health, particularly following the suicide of his son, Matthew, who battled depression and mental illness. He said:

"I'm not a professional counselor; I'm just a person who cares deeply. But I know what it's like to be in so much pain that you don't want to get out of bed in the morning". He further said, "Your illness is not your identity. Your chemistry is not your character." His wife, Kay Warren, said, "Depression is a massive monster that demands every ounce of your strength to keep it at bay."

Lysa TerKeurst, a well-known Christian author and president of Proverbs 31 Ministries, has shared her journey through depression, particularly during her battle with cancer and personal hardships.

She said, "Sometimes it takes an overwhelming breakdown to have an undeniable breakthrough. Depression doesn't wait for the right moment to come in. It just creeps up and starts to pull you under"

Charles Spurgeon, often referred to as the "Prince of Preachers," suffered from bouts of severe depression throughout his life, which he candidly discussed in his sermons and writings. He also said:

"I am the subject of depressions so fearful that I hope none of you ever get to such extremes of wretchedness as I go to." He further said, "I have sometimes been in the very depths of despondency, but at such times I have generally found comfort in the word of God and have been helped to rise above my sorrow."

The strength to exercise this authority and mastery over negative emotions will come from Zion, the presence of the Lord Jesus Christ. This is highlighted in Psalms 110:3 (AMPC), "The Lord will send forth from Zion the scepter of Your strength; rule, then, in the midst of Your foes".

However, our secular culture is gradually depleting our ability to connect to our real essence and spirituality. Recently, researchers conducted a scientific study on the correlation between depression and spirituality[1] . The study highlighted the fact that faith-based spiritual intervention has a significant impact in dealing with depression and associated effects.

We are not mere "bodies" trying to have a spiritual experience, but we are spirit beings attempting to have a "bodily" experience. You are more a spirit being than you think.

Life is a spiritual adventure. To live life without understanding this perspective can make one vulnerable and unstable. This is not suggesting that you live in a way that disconnects you from the realities of our days. But essentially, it is important to have a balanced perspective on life and living. Understanding our tripartite nature — that you are a spirit being with a soul and living in a body - and our ability to take care of our total self is very pivotal in living a stable and healthy life. Some people only focus on taking care of one aspect while neglecting others. What you feed grows

---

1. https://www.ncbi.nlm.nih.gov/pmc/articles/PMC104187 14/

and whatever you starve will die, it is only a matter of time. For instance, we have made tremendous progress in taking care of the body. What about the soul and spirit? The scripture admonishes us to pay attention to the welfare of your innermost being, for from there flows the wellspring of life (Proverbs 4:23b, TPT)

This book mainly focuses on how to guard and take care of the soul, which is the seat of our emotions. The soul is the integration of your mind, emotions, and will. It is the seat of your feelings, desires, affections, and aversions. The soul can experience joy or sorrow. David said in Psalms 35:9, "my soul shall be joyful in the Lord: it shall rejoice in his salvation". Towards His death, Jesus said 'my soul is exceedingly sorrowful' (Matthew 26:38) that means even Jesus shares these connections with us humans. The scriptures say Jesus wept (John 11:35). In another place, the scriptures state that we have a high priest who can be touched with the feelings of our infirmities (Hebrews 4:15). God said to Cain, 'why is your countenance fallen' (Genesis 4:6). In another place, the scriptures state that God felt sorry for making man and was grieved (Genesis 6:6). All these show that God can relate to our feelings and is concerned with the very health of our emotions that sit in the soulish realm.

In recent years, especially with the pandemic, depression has taken a severe toll on people, no matter who you are, believers and non—believers. Depression has been one of the greatest enemies of one's glorious destiny. It elevates hopelessness to the highest degree possible and isolates a person to destruction. Depression can incapacitate, demobilize, and rob one of freedom to be expressive of the potential embedded in us. But thanks be unto God who causes us to always, not sometimes, triumph in Christ, the Anointed One (paraphrased, 2 Corinthians 2:14).

This book draws essentially from the wisdom nuggets embedded in scriptures with practical examples of people who triumphed over the affliction of depression. Praise God, the bible has enough to offer in dealing with depression. I believe that as you read through this book, God will encounter you, bring His freedom, and empower you to provide support to those who are struggling with depression.

2

The incapacitating and overwhelming power of complaints

LAY ASIDE THE WEIGHT OF COMPLAINT

....I complained, and my spirit
was overwhelmed
Psalms 77:3b

C omplaints come from the feelings of powerlessness, help-lessness, and dissatisfaction about a situation and life. We gripe when we are upset and feel incapable of changing a situation.

Psalms 77:3b says "I complained, and my spirit was over-whelmed". The word "overwhelmed" connotes the idea of be-ing shrouded, clothed, enveloped, languished, weakened, and swooned. This overwhelming feeling puts weight upon the soul, envelopes us with negative emotions, and results in depression.

The bible says you cannot even add a cubit to your stature by complaining and griping. More often than not, people complain to get things off their chests and vent, and not necessarily to solve issues or create a change. How much of emotional energy do we waste by complaining about things we don't have the power to change. The vast majority of us complain about the weather. When it is cloudy, we become moody and when there is sunshine; we become elated. We have allowed things beyond our control to determine the states of our minds. Therefore, the change we need is definitely not out there but within; a change of mindset to simply accept things beyond our control, such as people's behaviors towards us, your late-arriving order, a flight delay because of weather, and so on.

The accumulation of frustrations sustained over time can put a weight on your emotions and mind. I remember reading an article about effective and ineffective complaining. The truth is that you don't want to relinquish too much power to things or people external to you. The question is how do I express my concerns without exhaustion?

Let it pass

For some things in life, we have to learn to let it pass. Not everything in your space requires a response or reaction. You have to begin to develop the capacity within you to let some things pass without affecting your emotions. Not every tweet or social media post requires your opinion. In life, there is a highway of peace where you simply choose your battles.

Jonathan Edwards made several resolutions that put him in a safe place where he can avoid people or situations for the sake of his own ease. For instance, he resolved never to allow, even in the least, emotions of anger toward irrational beings. Imagine Jesus Christ at the hour of the greatest trial and need, He should have complained when all His acquaintances left Him, abandoned by closest friends, relatives and even His God. The Bible says, 'He allowed them to pass and committed Himself to God who is able to save and deliver' (Hebrews 5:7-9, KJV).

The third perspective

There is so much value in seeking a third perspective before attacking or reacting to situations that want to put a weight on your emotions. In most cultures of the 21st century, most people believe they can figure out life by themselves with no support. They prefer to bottle things up, despite being surrounded by people who could provide authentic support. While I am not in support of addictive relationships, where we constantly need support and validation, a third perspective could help see situations differently and possibly prevent you from depleting precious emotional energy. We all can use the principle of the third perspective as a sounding box to have a more balanced viewpoint of situations. You may want to talk to trusted friends or family to gain a new perspective. Also, you can be intentional in building a supportive network with diverse groups of friends and acquaintances to provide objective viewpoints. The bottom line here is to avoid keeping issues within you. A problem shared is a problem halved solved. In a study conducted by Age UK in the United Kingdom, where three out of ten adults shared their worries about certain situations, 36% of these reported that they felt better, 26% felt relief and 8% showed that the problem went away once shared[1].

The Bible offers many examples of how genuine relationships can help us find strength, encouragement, and support. The scriptures say, "As iron sharpens iron, so a man sharpens the countenance of his friend (Proverbs 27:17, NKJV). This implies that trusted acquaintances can bring out a better version of you and can make you more effective. In 1 Samuel 23:16, the scriptures say that "And Jonathan, Saul's son, rose and went to David at Horesh, and strengthened his hand in God." No matter how strong we are or have become, we all need friends who can strengthen us in God.

Proverbs 27:9 says, "Oil and perfume make the heart glad, and the sweetness of a friend comes from his earnest counsel". This implies we can draw sweetness from the hearty counsel of a gen-

---

1.

https://www.ageuk.org.uk/latest-news/archive/share-proble ms-to-lighten-your-load/#:~:text=And%20the%20old%20ad age%20of,feel%20brighter%20as%20a%20result uine friend. The reality is that God has placed them all around you within your reach.

Engage the therapeutic power of time

There is an adage that says, "time heals all wounds" (maybe not all). With the passage of time, emotional turmoil, pain and suffering tend to fade and eventually people become better. Every now and then, when there is an issue, most people want to jump into a solution mode and fix the issue. However, most times they end up escalating the problem rather than resolving them. Somehow, when we allow time to take its full course, there seems to be a realignment of events that can dissolve the negative emotions and bad feelings we once had. Time can create a safe space, bring new alternatives, new sane people, and new perspectives into the picture. Time and patience can take care of certain things in life. Given enough time, we can have a clearer picture and a change of perspective about persons and situations.

In a proactive sense, how does one engage the therapeutic power of time? Do you just sit there and wait for a change of situation and feelings? That is what I will share in this entire book.

Engaging in something bigger than you

I watched a brief clip some time ago, and the speaker alluded to the fact that with mental wellness, there is a strong correlation between healing of the mind and a person's involvement in a cause greater than him or her. It is impossible to go past personal limitations without committing or serving something greater than you. Gloria Copeland once said, "if you think about yourself long enough, that is enough to cause depression". There is something special and thrilling about engaging in a task, cause or move that puts a demand on all dimensions of your life -spirit, soul and body. Such engagement puts a demand on your intellectual capacity with a physical exertion on your body.

To fill up ourselves with only your own needs and concerns brings no or very little satisfaction and fulfilment. I have discovered that people who invest in others and a vision greater than themselves often have a more balanced perspective on life and events around them. Think about how you can serve another person's vision, create a path for another to succeed, engage your creativity in solving a challenge, and the list goes on and on. When you extend yourself, you will begin to experience happiness and fulfillment at unprecedented levels. Jesus puts it this way after the servants have traded with their talents, He said enter into the joy of your Lord (Matthew 25:23, NKJV).

3

The therapeutic power of speaking to yourself

A CLOSED MOUTH IS A CLOSED DESTINY

Death and life are in the power of the tongue, and they who indulge in it shall eat the fruit of it [for death or life].
Proverbs 18:21 (AMPC)

We have allowed every person out there and social media platforms to speak constantly to us and our emotions. That is too much power relinquished to people who may not have your best interests at heart. But there is an enormous power when we decide to take charge and begin to speak to ourselves inwardly and audibly. A great therapeutic power can be released when we begin to speak to ourselves.

A closed mouth is a closed destiny. You are the most authentic prophet over your life. In fact, no matter how powerful the person speaking over your life is, you can cancel it by your own words. That is to show how much power is embedded in your words. Whether or not you know it, there is a continuous internal monologue that can dictate the state of our emotions. How you talk to yourself, whether internally or audibly, can either be beneficial, elevating your confidence, or destructive, eroding your self-worth.

Consistent negative self-talk can drag you down into a deep miry clay of depression and it can be hard to get back up. The good news is that there is a covenant pathway to breaking out of the cycle of negativity through His word.

Dig deep within - encourage yourself

David encouraged himself in the Lord (1 Samuel 30:6, NKJV), not in things or who was with him. No one is going to do this for you consistently. To depend on external encouragement or motivation all the time is equivalent to living on narcotics for daily survival, which is practically not sustainable. But you may wonder, how did he encourage himself in the Lord? What did he say if he ever said anything to himself? The scripture says he did it in the Lord. I believe he literary spoke to himself and reminded himself of his past dealings with God. He remembered the faithfulness of God in the past. Many times, people discard their past experiences with God, they forget about past victories. Your past successes can be a launching pad to face present day challenges. You can anchor your faith and hope on that, if God had ever delivered you in the past, he will do it again. He is the God of the again and still operates in cycles (1 Sam 3:21). In Psalms 77:3, David said, 'I will remember the years of the right hand of God, when God delivered me from the bears, lions, Saul's assault and family neglect'. In Psalms 27:10, he said, 'if my father and mother forsake me, the Lord will pick me up'.

The lesson here is that amid your self doubts and frustrations, you need to find a place in God when He delivered and brought you through hard situations. As you read this book, I would like to ask you a simple question: has God ever been faithful to you? This is where impactful self-talk begins. Start to talk to yourself about the faithfulness of God, how he has helped you in the past. It is an intentional effort to place a demand on your mind to do a recall.

This is a scripture I use for my personal self-talk -

"Why are you cast down, O my soul? And why are you disquieted within me? Hope in God; For I shall yet praise Him, The help of my countenance and my God" (Psalm 43:5). I use this scripture to speak to myself internally and audibly over my emotions. It has worked 100%. Now I need to emphasize here that self-talk is not just positive talk, it is scriptural self-talk. The mistake many people make is that they use their words in self-talk. Well, that could take you as far as any human solution can take you. But when you start using the scriptures, you release enormous power over your life and emotions.

Few scriptures here:

2 Peter 1:19 KJV, "We have also a more sure word of prophecy; whereunto ye do well that ye take heed, as unto a light that shineth in a dark place, until the day dawn, and the day star arise in your hearts:"

When you begin to declare the word over your life, it turns into a light that is able to pierce through darkness that the enemy wants to put over your life.

Acts 20:32 KJV, "And now, brethren, I commend you to God, and to the word of his grace, which is able to build you up, and to give you an inheritance among all them which are sanctified."

The word is able to build you up. It has an unlimited capacity to uplift and strengthen. The passion translation (paraphrased) says 'the word is all that you need to become strong'. By extrapolation, the word is your primary support system and all you need to become strong in all dimensions of realms. This is what I call Word-based confessional therapy.

Dealing with Shame and Secrecy

One devotional (Hope for every moment by Bishop T.D. Jakes) I used several years ago, which actually helped me during a tough time in life when I dealt with the heavy feelings of being ostracized by people I really trusted. He said something very instructive and I quote, "the very best of us camouflage the very worst in us with religious colloquialisms that reduce Christianity to more of an act than an attitude."

If you have dealt with assaults or have been a victim of abuse anytime, dealing with such events comes with a lot of shame, regrets and worst of all secrecy. Our societies do not deal well or know how to take care of these victims, and sadly, even within the church. So many victims resort to secrecy and isolation, which are one of the greatest weapons of the enemy. It takes a lot of boldness to accept healing in these sensitive areas of our lives. Generally, things that are covered don't heal well or fast.

Because most of these unfortunate circumstances affect the soul, which is not visible for the most part to human therapists. No matter how dark the situation could be, there is a covenant way out. The scripture says the word of God believed and declared can cut deep into the spirit and soul, ... and administer the necessary healings in those hidden places beyond the human sight. This is where there is a need for intentional re-programming with the word. Accepting what the word says, who the word says you are and what the word says you can do (Rom 12:2). Do not attempt to reprogram based on people's experiences alone. However, distorted experiences may lead to the continuation of the negative cycle. However, we have a more sure word of prophecy which is well tested and tried (2 Peter 1:19). Therefore, I would recommend reprograming with that more sure of word of prophesy, which carries the everlasting healing balm.

4

The law of rest

RECONNECT WITH YOUR TRUE ESSENCE

You will keep him in perfect peace, Whose
mind is stayed on You, Because he trusts in You.
Isaiah 26:3 (KJV)

Many people celebrate going on vacation to rest, which is by the way one of the ways to disconnect from the daily busy routines. I have also seen people return from vacation tired and exhausted. Rest is not a function of place, but a function of relationship. A healthy relationship with your true self and Christ Jesus. So whether or not you travel for a vacation, you can practice being restful. True rest can become a pavilion for the soul, serving as a wellspring for increasing creativity and a catalyst for development.

There is a dimension of spirituality which can help deal with depression that is rarely talked about. This is the dimension of faith that causes a believer to rest in the provisions of redemption in Christ and cease from toiling with human strength and intelligence.

We must constantly remind ourselves of the need to rest from all our works as God did. But what does that really mean to you and me? The Bible says God, the omnipotent One, rested and ceased from His works.

The entire chapter of Hebrews 4 is dedicated to the fact that there is a promise of rest for every believer. The question is why are believers depressed and restless? Before we go too far on this, let's look at Elijah, that mighty man of God who called down fire, slew the prophets of Baal, had great power with God to lock and unlock the heavens. But in 1 Kings 19:4, he was basically tired, lost hope temporarily, and wanted to die. So does that mean one can be anointed and depressed and have to deal with hopelessness?

The truth is that you can be engaged in a good course, firing on all cylinders and get exhausted without knowing it. That is why Jesus every now and then would depart to be alone with God. That was His custom. Jesus told His disciples after a successful kingdom adventure to come apart and rest. Once in a while, we need to isolate or hibernate from all the good stuff we have committed ourselves to. Intentional isolation for rejuvenation is required to keep us from depression. The danger you want to avoid is to be tired - mentally, physically, and emotionally and not know it. Elijah was probably tired and didn't know it.

Being in a restful state can also imply being present in the now. In an attempt to plan for the future with all scenario simulations, which is fantastic, however, one could get caught up in such activities and lose the richness and depth of each passing moment. Staying mindful of the present is an intentional activity that can cultivate the soul with the beauty of the present moment. We all have legitimate justification to keep engaging with the activities and chaos of the modern life just like Martha. Look at what Jesus said to her in Luke 10:40-42:

"40 But Martha was distracted with much serving, and she approached Him and said, "Lord, do You not care that my sister has left me to serve alone? Therefore, tell her to help me."

41 And Jesus answered and said to her, "Martha, Martha, you are worried and troubled about many things. 42 But one thing is needed, and Mary has chosen that good part, which will not be taken away from her."

Much serving distracted Martha, and she missed a divine opportunity embedded in the moment. A lot of us are like Martha, "worried and troubled about many things" and this has a strong tendency to put a weight on the soul affecting our mental health. But intentional investment in building our faith is a guaranteed covenant gateway to rest and Isaiah 26:3 confirms that "You will keep him in perfect peace, Whose mind is stayed on You". Just like Mary in Luke 10:42, Jesus said, "Mary has chosen that good part, which will not be taken away from her."

5

The impact of entertainment on emotional balance and behavior

GUARD YOUR SOUL

Finally, brethren, whatsoever things are true, whatsoever things are honest, whatsoever things are just, whatsoever things are pure, whatsoever things are lovely, whatsoever things are of good report; if there be any virtue, and if there be any praise, think on these things.
Philippians 4:8 (KJV)

Most people have used entertainment as a way of escape and source of comfort and ease during times of distress, like we saw during the COVID-19 pandemic. The subscription to streaming platforms increased significantly as many sought solace.

Entertainment can stir up different emotions depending on the type. You know, somehow our minds are being conditioned to always want entertainment, as if it is the medication we need for survival.

There are definitely benefits of entertainment on mental health, such as listening to favorite music and comedies, which could be great for managing stress and distract people from their present discomfort.

There has been an ongoing discussion on how to use entertainment as a means of therapy. A typical example is the music therapy programs used to help people with mental health issues, such as depression, stress disorders, and anxiety.

A quick caution here: as believers, we must understand that music is very spiritual. Every music has its source of inspiration, whether from God or Satan. Any music will take you to where it came from.

Look at satan's ministry before his fall, in Ezekiel 28:13, "Thou hast been in Eden the garden of God; every precious stone was thy covering, the sardius, topaz, and the diamond, the beryl, the onyx, and the jasper, the sapphire, the emerald, and the carbuncle, and gold: the workmanship of thy tabrets and of thy pipes was prepared in thee in the day that thou was created."

So, from the moment of his creation, he possessed the innate ability to be a musician. His vocal cords (pipes) were divinely crafted to sing and worship Adonai. But he corrupted his gift and every inspiration he gives cannot help except to further corrupt.

That is why we must be very careful about the kinds of music we expose ourselves to.

There is no doubt that music is therapeutic. Look at the case of Saul. Whenever the evil spirit comes to torment him, as David played with the anointing God gave him, the evil spirit lifted from Saul. That is how powerful, anointed music and songs can be. They can drive out evil spirits of depression, stress disorders, and anxiety.

Installing Entertainment Guardrails

This is not about being dogmatic or being rigid, but about creating a safe space for yourself and operating within the acceptable perimeter that ensures your vulnerability is not being exploited by the enemy. Just like physical guardrails on roads help to avoid accidents, entertainment guardrails can be a pivotal proactive step in protecting our mental health from overindulgence in an increasingly digitized world.

In Proverbs 25:28, the scripture says, "He that hath no rule over his own spirit is like a city that is broken down, and without walls." This implies that if you simply allow everything online to come into space, one is compared to a city without walls, everything goes in the name of entertainment. You will not only suffer from entertainment overload, but a feeling of emptiness from excessive screen time. Certain movies and video games can trigger fear and feelings of aggression.

Another important guardrail is the ability to balance real world and digital interactions intentionally. I remember traveling and watching a young man stuck to his phone throughout the flight duration. Is it wrong to do that on a flight? Absolutely not. However, that experience has denied him of the possibility of a rich experience of camaraderie that comes through social interactions with others. I am deeply concerned that digital entertainment is rapidly replacing meaningful real-world interactions and experiences that can nurture our mental health and resilience, reducing the risk of social isolation and loneliness that have the propensity of increasing depression tendencies.

As Spirit filled believers, every now and then, the Holy Spirit gives a check in our spirits when we are over-consuming digital contents, but many times we choose to ignore His voice. This reminds me of Galatians 5:17, which underscores the reality of the struggle between the lust of the flesh and the Spirit. Many people don't know is a brutal fight between the inordinate desires of the flesh and the dynamic life of the Spirit . To continue to harden one's conscience towards the prompting of the Holy Spirit is walking on a slippery slope at one's own peril. This sounds harsh, right? But this is how many good believers have entered a pit of depression by constantly ignoring His voice.

Let me show you another perspective on how to deal with excessive cravings for entertainment that could ruin one's mental space if unchecked. Paul, that great Apostle, look at how he chose to handle the cravings of the flesh in 1 Cor 9:27 AMPC, "27 But [like a boxer] I buffet my body [handle it roughly, discipline it by hardships] and subdue it, for fear that after proclaiming to others the Gospel and things pertaining to it, I myself should become unfit [not stand the test, be unapproved and rejected as a counterfeit]". He said I buffet my body, handle it roughly, deny it of the possibility of expressing its base desires. That is how serious the fight is in indulging the flesh with excessive entertainment.

6

Be comfortable in your skin

BE YOURSELF, NEVER WISH YOU WERE SOMEONE ELSE

14 I will praise thee; for I am fearfully and wonderfully made:
marvellous are thy works; and that my soul knoweth right well.
15 My substance was not hid from thee, when I was made in secret,
and curiously wrought in the lowest parts of the earth.
Psalms 139:14-15 (KJV)

We live in the days where people desperately want to become someone else. They wish they were different and constantly strive to assume another person's posture and personality. This is not about becoming a better version of themselves, but more about a feeling of insecurity about themselves, which can negatively impact one's mental health.

This is a very sensitive subject and so I will not give particular examples to buttress my point. But a particular shout out to our mothers and wives with their beautiful stretch marks. This should not stress you out and don't try to get rid of them. You are already a model because those marks are proofs of where you have been, what you have survived and that you have passed through the valley of shadow of death and still made it alive. So rejoice in God for His mighty deliverance and we are eternally grateful to God for you.

The point here is, one of the reasons for depression in our days is that people are losing confidence in their identity and constantly engaging in internal struggles. Embracing who God has made you to be empowers you to look within and explore capabilities God has placed within you. Some wish they had other people's gifts and callings and therefore ignore their own. If you ask them, they feel God is unfair for giving them no gifts or their gifts are inferior to others. The bible says let everyone abide in his or her calling (1 Corinthians 7:20).

In 1 Corinthians 12:7, the scriptures say, "But the manifestation of the Spirit is given to every man to profit withal." The truth from this scripture is that every man or woman is gifted according to the divine programing in the kingdom. In fact, Romans 12:6 says our gifts differ from one another according to the grace of God given to us. You do not need someone to validate or approve your giftings. There is no gift that is superior or inferior, but we are each graced differently, which reflects the manifold wisdom of God.

Being comfortable in your skin is a process and journey of self-acceptance, awareness, discovery, and expression.

Embrace your person and physicality

There are some people who don't have the courage to even look at themselves in the mirror. They feel so insecure about what they see in the mirror and that's causing a lot of negative emotions. Look at Psalms 139:14-15 (KJV) closely.

Psalms 139:14 I will praise thee; for I am fearfully and wonderfully made: marvelous are thy works; and that my soul knoweth right well.

Psalms 139:15 My substance was not hid from thee, when I was made in secret, and curiously wrought in the lowest parts of the earth.

The Psalmist describes the wonder of your birth, showing you were intricately and curiously designed. There is a mystery about your physicality such that you have to be looked at and studied. You should celebrate and appreciate your unique nature. You are so uniquely crafted that you don't have a duplicate. A Flawless Being designed the way you smile, laugh, walk and even your shape. Your inner self ought to know it and appreciate this so well. You are a masterpiece. Depending on external sources to validate this makes you very vulnerable.

There is so much pressure out there to conform your physicality to a certain mode, expectations, and standards, some of which are very unrealistic.

Ephesians 2:10 says we are God's handiwork created with purpose and intentionality. God intentionally designed everything about you to fulfill a specific purpose and assignment. Trying to become someone else implies that you may be missing in action in the big picture and grand scheme of things predestined by God.

This is not by any means saying that you cannot improve or look after yourself. It is simply accepting things you cannot change about yourself. I will waste a lot of emotional energy wishing I looked like someone else. This is one way the enemy has held many people captive to unattainable expectations and that can negatively affect self-esteem, worth and mental health.

Your identity is from Him, not in anything else

The struggle with identity is very real. Identity crisis is one of the leading causes of depression and anxiety. Identity crisis will make you question and doubt your assignment, calling, purpose, personality, and values.

Who am I? What is my worth? Why am I here? What is my purpose and calling? How do I find my role and purpose within the larger context? Answering these pertinent questions with certainty is essential to escape from identity crises. Don't be scared to ask yourself these questions because they can provide an opportunity for growth and the greatest discovery of a lifetime. Jesus asked His disciples, "who do men say that I am (Matthew 16:13)? A lot of us go around everywhere and on social media platforms asking the same question, who am I really? Now to do this without first knowing who you are really, or an inner awareness is the most disastrous thing to do in the world. This will make you most vulnerable and at the mercy of people's myopic view about you. You may end up restricting yourself to a very narrowed view and limited possibilities.

Few Scriptural provisions that address your identity

Acts 17:28 TPT says, "It is through him that we live and function and have our identity; just as your own poets have said, 'Our lineage comes from him.'"

If you are looking for who you really are, look no further. Your identity is in God, your maker. According to the scriptures, He is the source of our being and identity. When you know that your identity is from God, you pursue Him with vigor and determination. The knowledge of our identity and potential resides within God's omniscience.

Genesis 1:27 "So God created mankind in his own image, in the image of God created he him; male and female created he them."

This image has little or nothing to do with our physicality. It is more of a spiritual nature and character. So God's original intent is to share His nature and character with mankind, male and female. No wonder in Psalms 82:6, the scripture refers to us as gods, God's representative to execute judgement on His behalf. That is huge! Let this galvanize your thinking and self-perception about who you are.

Revelation 5:10 (KJV) "And hast made us unto our God kings and priests: and we shall reign on the earth."

Can you fathom the fact that Christ redeemed us to become kings and priests to God? You have royalty in your spiritual DNA, at your core. He did not stop there. God wants you and me to reign on the earth. That is our identity. Think kingly and priestly thoughts!

Every word is confirmed in the mouth of two or three witnesses. See 1 Peter 2:9, "But ye are a chosen generation, a royal priesthood, a holy nation, a peculiar people; that ye should shew forth the praises of him who hath called you out of darkness into his marvellous light." Another translation says, 'you are priests who are kings!'. This implies that you have been ordained to reign over a domain and a sphere of influence. Whenever the enemy wants you to doubt your identity, just open your bible to 1 Peter 2:9 and read it aloud until you drown out that negative voice.

In Psalm 36:9, the scriptures says "For with thee is the fountain of life: in thy light shall we see light."

That implies, in God, there is a light potential that enables us to receive the light of a revelation of who we are and our essence.

It is also interesting to note that in Christ, our identity is linked to the Abrahamic lineage.

Galatians 3:29 "And if ye be Christ's, then are ye Abraham's seed, and heirs according to the promise."

What is so unique about being Abraham's seed or offspring? As a descendant of Abraham, you are ordained to possess the gates or cities of your enemies (Genesis 22:17-18, KJV). Another translation says they shall defeat their enemies. That implies you are not permitted to be defeated by your enemies, including depression.

Jesus said concerning the woman that was bound by the spirit of infirmity in Luke 13:16 "And ought not this woman, being a daughter of Abraham, whom Satan hath bound, lo, these eighteen years, be loosed from this bond on the sabbath day?" The children of Abraham are not permitted to be bound by depression. Those who know who they are in the covenant shall be strong and they shall do exploits (Daniel 11:32b)

Your identity was never designed to be tied to performance and achievement

Our identity is never supposed to be tied to our performance and achievements. To do that is to bring yourself under intense pressure and the need to constantly perform to an audience that may not be paying attention to you. This could be one reason some people keep pursuing different adventures, whether or not relevant to their destiny, because of the addictive nature of achievement. This tendency increases a person's insecurity and warps our sense of worth in life. Further, it creates an appetite for unhealthy competition, leading to anxiety, depression, and other mental health issues.

Look at what God said about Jesus even before He performed any miracle in Matthew 3:17 "And lo a voice from heaven, saying, This is my beloved Son, in whom I am well pleased". God, the Father, giving His approval before any demonstration of power. Many people think our performance moves God, and He is only pleased with us when we perform or become a celebrity. That is a big lie from the pit of hell. While achievements are wonderful, the question is what would happen if, for whatever reason, you could no longer perform or no longer be on the center stage?

In Acts 8, there was a man named Simon the Sorcerer who held a whole city captive by his sorcery and everyone in the city of Samaria considered him a great power of God. He was a local celebrity in Samaria.

Acts 8:9-11 says, "But there was a certain man called Simon, who previously practiced sorcery in the city and astonished the people of Samaria, claiming that he was someone great. 10 to whom they all gave heed, from the least to the greatest, saying, 'This man is the great power of God.' 11 And they heeded him because he had astonished them with his sorceries for a long time."

But when a higher power came to town heralded by Philip, and displaced him, he quickly got converted. Wrapping your identity around performance is dangerous. When he saw Peter demonstrate the power of God, he offered him money in exchange to get that power in order to recover his position and identity. Acts 8:18-19 illustrates this,

"18 And when Simon saw that through the laying on of the apostles' hands the Holy Spirit was given, he offered them money, 19 saying, "Give me this power also, that anyone on whom I lay hands may receive the Holy Spirit."

Simon focused on himself, performance, and regaining control of influence again. Such a person who is constantly driven by prestige and performance will be desperate to always be on the hit list of the highest achievers. If, for whatever reason, the spotlight is no longer on you, will that affect who you are at the core or affect your self-worth? This is one reason many celebrities are miserable because they constantly exhaust themselves in the pursuit of fame and human applause, trying to keep up with the pace. In fact, this connection could be linked to family experiences where love is tied to performance and the achievement of good grades at school. It is time to free yourself from enslavement and burn out of performance.

There is what the bible calls 'good success' in Joshua 1:8, that implies there could be a 'bad success'. Any achievement or success, so to speak, that leaves you empty; bankrupt of emotional strength and stability is a "bad success". Never pursue success as a platform to increase your self-worth or esteem at the expense of your emotional well-being, values, and fulfillment.

7

The power of community & association

NEVER TRAVEL ALONE

9 Two are better than one; because they have a good reward for their labour.

10 For if they fall, the one will lift up his fellow: but woe to him that is alone when he falleth; for he hath not another to help him up.

Ecclesiastes 4:9-10 (KJV)

One of the most potent tools the enemy uses to keep people bound in depression is isolation. I mean unwanted and unhealthy isolation. Isolation itself is not a bad thing when you intentionally separate yourself to seek God. Proverbs 18:1 KJV, says "Through desire a man, having separated himself, seeketh and intermeddleth with all wisdom." Sometimes it is required that we separate ourselves for a deeper fellowship with God without distractions.

Social isolation does not always imply being physically disconnected from a circle or a group of people. One can have a feeling of isolation within a group or even in relationships when perspectives are conflicting or there is no joint interest. Also, this happens when there is a feeling that members of a group won't understand you. The natural instinct would be to withdraw into yourself and become a cave man or woman like Elijah in 1 Kings 19:9.

Breaking free from the vicious cycle of isolation is pivotal to overcome depression. In some remote places where there is no access to electricity, people make fire by gathering sticks in a bunch. Whenever you isolate a log of wood from the bunch, it is only a matter of time before that log loses its power to burn and produce heat. An African proverb says it is easy to break a broomstick, but not a bunch. It is a known fact that lions never travel alone, they move, hunt, and exist in prides. It is hard to defeat them in their prides. That is how God has designed us to live. Everything within our ecosystem was designed to function and operate cooperatively with symbiotic interactions.

A very important highlight here is that the danger of isolation is a much greater risk than the vulnerability of intimacy.

Dealing with isolation the scriptural way

Open your mind

Minds are like parachutes; they work best when they are opened. Nobody will do it for you. Because isolation starts from the mind, your deliverance will have to start from the mind too. The vulnerability of intimacy demands that you must be willing to trust God with your life, the processes He is taking you through and the people He is bringing into and taking away from your life. Open your mind to the scriptural platforms He is providing for you, such as fellowship. Reading this book, you may have had an unpleasant experience with friendships and groups, including churches. That should not make you close your mind and deny yourself the possibility of finding the right one. We thrive within the context of associations where there is a mutual interest. Even from the natural standpoint, you cannot be fruitful by yourself alone. Fruitfulness demands interaction and intimacy.

Before you rush out there to look for groups where you share common interests, let me point you to the foundation of having a meaningful fellowship and relationship out there.

A healthy external relationship depends on a robust internal fellowship between yourself and God. When we spend quality time with God, it enriches our perspectives and helps us bring a sense of serenity and fulfillment into our interactions with others. We can show up in our external relationships with a strong sense of authenticity that can foster genuine connections based on trust and mutual understanding.

1 John 1:3 says, "That which we have seen and heard declare we unto you, that ye also may have fellowship with us: and truly our fellowship is with the Father, and with his Son Jesus Christ."

When you shut yourself in with God in surrender and your devotion, you provide yourself with the opportunity to interact with Him and Jesus. We serve a God who wants to talk and relate with us intimately. But we prefer to talk to every other person apart from Him.

Isaiah 1:18 says, "Come now, and let us reason together, says the Lord. Though your sins are like scarlet, they shall be as white as snow; though they are red like crimson, they shall be like wool." He sends an invitation to you. He says "Come now, and let us reason together". As we continue to ignore His invitation for interaction, we will continue to go round in circles searching for intimacy, which makes us vulnerable to manipulation.

God asked Cain in Genesis 4:6 AMPC, "Why are you angry? And why do you look sad and depressed and dejected?" It shows the kind of God He is. He values relationships and cares how we feel. I need to ask someone reading this book, why do you keep running from God?

Another level of relationship (I know there are so many out there, but I am not a relationship coach!) I would like to address is your relationship with the Church. There is a mystery about the church that many are yet to discover. Have you had an unpleasant encounter with church people? Oh yes, I have too, with unpleasant stories. The church is not an organization but a spiritual organism. You and I must relate to the Church with a revelation based on the word of God.

Our spiritual life can be enhanced and preserved through fellowship with believers. Are there fake and hypocritical believers in the church? Oh for sure, but the presence of fake is an evidence there might be some genuine ones that you can leverage. Where did the disciples go when they were threatened not to preach in the name of Jesus?

Acts 4:23-24

"23 And being let go, they went to their own company, and reported all that the chief priests and elders had said unto them.

24 And when they heard that, they lifted up their voice to God with one accord, and said, Lord, thou art God, which hast made heaven, and earth, and the sea, and all that in them is:"

The scriptures say they went to their own company? Have you got any company? Who are your associates and confidants? Do you have people in your life that can call down heaven and the power of God? This is the Apostolic way and scriptural prescription to handling life challenges, struggles and the forces threatening us, including depression.Look at the outcome in Acts 4:31, "And when they had prayed, the place was shaken where they were assembled together; and they were all filled with the Holy Ghost, and they spake the word of God with boldness." There is a dimension in God that can only be assessed when we come together under a corporate unction to deal with the adversary and he does not stand a chance. Battles can be won easily through divine associations.

Look at Moses, the one who spoke to God face-to-face when Israel fought against the Amalekites led by Joshua, in Exodus 17:11-12–

"11 And it came to pass, when Moses held up his hand, that Israel prevailed: and when he let down his hand, Amalek prevailed.

12 But Moses' hands were heavy; and they took a stone, and put it under him, and he sat thereon; and Aaron and Hur stayed up his hands, the one on the one side, and the other on the other side; and his hands were steady until the going down of the sun."

Israel only prevailed as long as Moses' hands were lifted, showing the power of having someone petitioning God on your behalf. However, his hands got wearied and needed extra support. Aaron and Hur had to provide extra support to stabilize his hands. The truth is, we can only go so far by ourselves. However, to go farther and win some serious battles, such as depression, you need believers who will lift you in prayers. But you need to open up and ask for help. This type of vulnerability is far better than the risk of isolation.

This is one reason the Bible says in Hebrews 10:25 "Not forsaking the assembling of ourselves together, as the manner of some is; but exhorting one another: and so much the more, as ye see the day approaching."

Don't let the hurt of the past and misrepresentation of the Church deny you of the enormous power you can generate through the company of believers. This is one of our strongholds in the covenant to overcoming depression.

Jesus' model of association

Jesus Christ our Lord, while on earth, had different levels of relationships with people around Him—the three (Peter, James & John), the 12 apostles, 70 disciples and the multitude. He developed deep and meaningful relationships across different levels of relationships, showing a profound understanding of human connection and community. He gave a working model on how to prioritize relationships and fellowships for shared support. Look at how He handled the multitude in John 2:23-25. This group will fall into social medial classification in our days.

John 2:23-25

"23 Now when he was in Jerusalem at the passover, in the feast day, many believed in his name, when they saw the miracles which he did.

24 But Jesus did not commit himself unto them, because he knew all men,

25 And needed not that any should testify of man: for he knew what was in man."

Jesus would not trust or commit Himself to the multitude. He recognized their susceptibility to manipulation. Neither did He call them into His bosom, nor into deep communion with them. He was aware of their inconstancy and fickleness to move in a direction that pleased them. The question is why should you entrust your life and happiness to the fickleness on the social media?

Before His crucifixion and close to the darkest hour, He took the three who were His close confidants to pray and experience the most intimate experience with His Father.

Matthew 26:36-37

"36 Then cometh Jesus with them unto a place called Gethsemane, and saith unto the disciples, Sit ye here, while I go and pray yonder."

"37 And he took with him Peter and the two sons of Zebedee and began to be sorrowful and very heavy."

We ought to model our lives after this pattern to survive not only the demands of our calling but life challenges, including waging war against depression. There ought to be people in your life that you can share your struggles with without shame or fear of judgement. That is a key covenant escape route. If Jesus needed it, you and I would need it more. This is not only required during challenges but during times of triumphs and victories to keep you balanced on your perspectives. Jesus showed this also when He took the three to the mount of transfiguration.

Matthew 17:1-2

"1 And after six days Jesus taketh Peter, James, and John his brother, and bringeth them up into an high mountain apart, 2 And was transfigured before them: and his face did shine as the sun, and his raiment was white as the light."

These boundary conditions, mountaintop and valley experiences, need intimate relationships to maintain sanity and equilibrium in our mental health state.

8

Engaging the stronghold of blood of Jesus for triumph

THE BLOOD OF JESUS STILL SPEAKS

And they overcame him by the blood of the Lamb, and by the word of their testimony; and they loved not their lives unto the death.
Revelation 12:11 (KJV)

Life is very spiritual and to lose sight of this truth is to live at the mercy of the whims and caprices of the enemy of your soul. Psalms 74:20 says there are places on the earth that are habitations of cruelty. The cruelty of anxiety and depression are constantly being perpetrated by forces of evil. In Ephesians 2:2, the bible calls the chief of these forces *the prince of the power of the air*. Another translation says he is "*dark ruler of the earthly realm who fills the atmosphere with his authority & influence*". He likes to fill and control the atmospheric condition with darkness, oppression, and depression. So, it is a battle of who controls the atmosphere.

The Bible refers to depression as a "spirit of heaviness" that sits upon the souls, which is the seat of our emotions. Let me show you another place in the scripture that talks about this "oppressive and depressive force".Look at it In Zechariah 1:21, "Then said I, What come these to do? And he spake, saying, These are the horns which have scattered Judah, so that no man did lift up his head: but these are come to fray them, to cast out the horns of the Gentiles, which lifted up their horn over the land of Judah to scatter it.".

The ultimate agenda of this force of heaviness is to scatter your emotions, thinking, perspective and would make sure that your head is not lifted in joy and exuberance.

2 Corinthians 10:3 further gives an excellent picture of how these forces operate to mess up your mental space and health.

The bible says here that "For though we walk (live) in the flesh, we are not carrying on our warfare according to the flesh and using mere human weapons" (2 Corinthians 10:3, AMPC)

This scripture implies there's a warfare over your entire life, including your emotional stability. The enemy doesn't want you and I to operate in a safe mental space. Again, the weapons of warfare should not be limited to just physical and scientific measures. If you do that as a believer, you are simply underutilizing covenant rights and privileges.Personally, whenever I am fighting against something, I declare it a street fight. Depending on the neighborhood you grew up in, if you have ever seen a street fight, the people involved use everything at their disposal - a log of wood, shoes, and everything they can grab. That is what makes it a street fight, no rules, but just win. In the fight against your mental health, declare a street fight.

2 Corinthians 10:4, AMPC "For the weapons of our warfare are not physical [weapons of flesh and blood], but they are mighty before God for the overthrow and destruction of strongholds. Take note of the word "strongholds". In this context, it represents arguments and reasonings. This implies that these strongholds exist in the mind (influencing our thought pattern). The enemy tries to take people captive in their minds, in the soul's realm.

If you look closely at 2 Corinthians 10:5 "[Inasmuch as we] refute arguments and theories and reasonings and every proud and lofty thing that sets itself up against the [true] knowledge of God; and we lead every thought and purpose away captive into the obedience of Christ (the Messiah, the Anointed One)" "

The scripture talks about arguments, theories and reasonings that want to challenge your mental balance. The question is, where are they coming from? I believe every thought has a source. Ephesians 2 talks about the prince of the power of the air. He is responsible for those whisperings that challenge your joy. He gives you reasons why you should be moody and not enjoy all the goodness around your life, the incremental progress you are making, and celebrate your small wins.

This is why the fight over your mental health is not just scientific, but deeply spiritual. For someone reading this book, you may have been slipping in and out of depression for years. The enemy does not open his prison door easily. He likes to perpetrate afflictions across generations. Maybe you have had a family history of depression, but there is certainly a covenant way out.

2 Corinthians 10:6 says, "Being in readiness to punish every [insubordinate for his] disobedience, when your own submission and obedience are fully secured and complete."

This scripture shows us our responsibility to punish every disobedience, the thoughts and reasonings that want to violate your mental space. But how is this supposed to be done?

I call this escape route *"the covenant escape via the blood of Jesus"*.

What is in the blood of Jesus that can destroy the hold of depression?

The Church, to a large extent, has downplayed the importance and breakthrough power in the blood of Jesus. We have been taught all kinds of sophisticated mechanisms to deal with depression, but most believers have not been taught the efficacy of the blood covenant in Christ Jesus. Most of the preaching today focuses on psychology, centering on self-worth and acceptance, which is not bad. However, to sustain our victory in God over every operation of satan, we must have the revelation of the immense power that is in the blood of Jesus. It is high time we went back to the fundamentals of our faith and victory in Christ Jesus.

In Hebrews 9:14, the Bible says "How much more shall the blood of Christ, who through the eternal Spirit offered himself without spot to God, purge your conscience from dead works to serve the living God?". If the blood can purge or cleanse the conscience, which is the voice of the soul, don't you think the same blood has the power to deliver the soul from depression? The blood of Jesus is a divine agent that opens up the heart and soul to new possibilities.

Leviticus 17:11B says 'it is the blood that makes atonement for the soul'.One connotation of the word atonement in this context implies a covering or the ability to purge and cleanse. The blood of Jesus is our wrap around shield of protection. This suggests that blood is capable of providing the soul (mind, emotions) with a shield against the assaults of depression. In Genesis 3:21, when Adam and Eve fell into sin and became naked and vulnerable, there was no better covering than the blood skin of an innocent animal. However, this power is only released through faith in the blood of Jesus (Romans 5:9).A quick call out on Adam's disposition, he had to disrobe himself and remove the covering of the leaves, which would not last long, before he could receive the covering provided by God. Today, many of us are trying to provide ourselves with alternate coverings apart from the blood with things such as work, addictive relationships, drugs, anger, resentment and the like. It is time to disrobe and take what God provides as a covering, the Blood of Jesus.

The blood of Jesus is the most potent remedy for the afflictions of the soul. So the blood of Jesus is not just to cleanse us from sin, but it has the capacity to deliver and provide a covering. It is high time we began to deploy and operate the full power of the blood of Jesus. There's enough power in the blood of Jesus to give us victory against anything satan throws at us.

The blood of Jesus is one of our surest strongholds in the covenant, as highlighted in Zechariah 9:11-12.

Zechariah 9:11-12

11 "As for you also, Because of the blood of your covenant, I will set your prisoners free from the waterless pit."

12 "Return to the stronghold, You prisoners of hope. Even today I declare That I will restore double to you."

Inherent in the blood of Jesus is a power to set prisoners free from every form of affliction, trauma, and captivity. There are people reading this book that have been hearing strange voices speaking condemnation, hopelessness and worthlessness over your identity and entire life. I have good news for you. We also have the speaking blood in the covenant. The Blood of Jesus Speaks! it speaks life, hope, forgiveness, redemption and recovery over every mental affliction.

Hebrews 12:24 AMPC, says "And to Jesus, the Mediator (Go-between, Agent) of a new covenant, and to the sprinkled blood which speaks [of mercy], a better and nobler and more gracious message than the blood of Abel [which cried out for vengeance]".

So the blood speaks mercy and can cancel out the contrary voice of condemnation, shame, and guilt. If I were you, I would begin to plead the blood of Jesus over mind, thinking and the entire soul. Reclaim the health of your soul by the blood of Jesus. You have to open your mouth and declare healing and health by the blood of Jesus over your soul. Oh, the blood still speaks today! The blood of Jesus has a voice that speaks in the spirit realm. It is testifying to

God and all forces in the realm of the spirit that you belong to God through the sacrifice of Jesus. But you have to appropriate what the blood is speaking over your life, otherwise the enemy won't lose his grip on your life. You can't beat thought with another thought, you beat a negative thought with words, not just your words, but declare what the blood of Jesus bought for you. For instance, you can declare that you have forgiveness (Colossians 1:14), sanctification (Hebrews 13:12), redemption (Ephesians 1:7), and justification (Romans 5:8-9)

Psalm 81:10 says, "I am the Lord thy God, which brought thee out of the land of Egypt: open thy mouth wide, and I will fill it."

Open your mouth and apply the speaking blood over your life.

Revelation 12:11 says, "And they overcame him by the blood of the Lamb and by the word of their testimony, and they did not love their lives to the death".

This implies that to overcome, you have to combine the Blood of Jesus with the utterance of your testimony. Declare repeatedly what the blood is speaking and has bought for you. Take your authority by the blood of Jesus and declare that not one day will the enemy have dominion over your thoughts, emotions and every aspect of your life.

A song writer said "My hope is built on nothing less, Than Jesus' blood and righteousness". Every believer must know how to take advantage of the life-giving blood of Jesus to maintain our mental dignity and destroy any form of bondage trying to hold us down.The blood of Jesus has the power to invigorate and restore the soul that sin has lacerated and destroyed. The blood of Jesus is God's antidote to the plague of depression that is ravaging the minds and souls of both young and old across all cultures. You can plead or apply the blood of Jesus over your emotions, thinking and your entire soul and demand that the force of depression lose its grip over your life.

You ought to rejoice about what the blood of Jesus provides–the redemption, deliverance, freedom and covering. Don't limit your joy and rejoicing to tangible stuff - the car, job, house and other material things. If you do that, you make yourself more vulnerable because then the enemy can attack these things and make your life miserable. But when you start rejoicing in what the blood has done and can do, you shatter the weight of depression that the enemy is attempting to place on your life. Exodus 12:13 says, "And the blood shall be to you for a token upon the houses where ye area and when I see the blood, I will pass over you, and the plague shall not be upon you to destroy you, when I smite the land of Egypt".

The plague could not come upon the children of Israel because of the blood. We all need to learn how to place our joy and confidence literally in a place that cannot be compromised, which is in the blood covenant.

Engaging the power of the blood through the holy communion

How else can we engage the blood covenant to overcome depression? We can also engage the blood covenant through the communion table to overcome every oppression of the devil. It will take revelation and spiritual understanding to unleash the supernatural power embedded in the holy communion when taken in faith. It is the most potent meal on the earth today that can secure the total health.

Our Lord Jesus said in John 6:56-57: "56 He that eateth my flesh, and drinketh my blood, dwelleth in me, and I in him. 57 As the living Father hath sent me, and I live by the Father: so he that eateth me, even he shall live by me".

You cannot dwell in Him and He in you, and still cohabit with the oppression of depression. One of the things that taking the communion does is to remind us that the blood already bought our total freedom. It reinforces our covenant consciousness by walking in the victory that the blood has purchased for us. It is important that we allow the revelation of this truth to sink into our conscious and subconscious mind.

The great Apostle of faith, Smith Wigglesworth, took communion every day, acknowledging that Christ's accomplishments on the cross served as a powerful antidote against pride. In fact, some have alluded to the fact that the secret to his sound health was that he took communion daily at the dining table. The important lesson here is that the same communion can serve as an antidote to anything evil in your life, including depression. The communion is not an ordinance to be observed randomly or occasionally, but to be observed continuously.

What the communion does is to keep fresh in our minds what Jesus Christ did for us on the cross. It keeps Isaiah 53:4 real as we celebrate His grace in our redemption and freedom over every form of darkness, including depression.

Isaiah 53:4 AMPC, says Surely He has borne our griefs (sicknesses, weaknesses, and distresses) and carried our sorrows and pains [of punishment], yet we [ignorantly] considered Him stricken, smitten, and afflicted by God [as if with leprosy].

The question is why should you continue to bear sicknesses, weaknesses, and distresses, including depression, when Christ has already borne it? The enemy we are dealing with is a rebel, and he wants to continue violating divine ordinances and provisions in redemption. But it is our duty to continue to enforce what Christ obtained for us in redemption. The communion gives us the opportunity to enforce our freedom from all distresses. As you take the communion elements, you open your mouth and declare that His death is life for you, the chastisement of our peace was upon him; and with his stripes, we were healed.

9

Cry out!

HELP IS ON THE WAY

When I cry unto thee, then shall mine enemies turn back: this I know;
for God is for me.
Psalm 56:9 (KJV)

Some are just too cute to cry out to God for help. They worry about their makeup and masculinity, and feel embarrassed to cry out. It is not just feminine to cry, even the bible says Jesus Wept! (John 11:35). The all-powerful and mighty Jesus wept. In another place, Jesus cried out to the Father, "My God, my God, why hast thou forsaken me"? (Matthew 27:46). The Amplified translation says "My God, My God, why have You abandoned Me [leaving Me helpless, forsaking and failing Me in My need]?". It is not lack of faith, neither is it a sign of weakness when you cry out to God.

From the natural and scientific standpoint, it is said that crying can provide support both to the body and mind by activating parasympathetic nervous system to help one self-soothe.[1] So science identifies crying as a way to release negative energy from your system.

From the scriptural perspective, the power of a sincere and heartfelt cry of faith is an unmatchable force in the covenant. To cry means to summon, invite, and call for help. When you direct your cry towards God, He pays attention. He never neglects the cry of His children. He still hears the desperate call and summons of someone who has nothing else to lose. Desperate people do desperate things, including crying out to God.

Psalm 56:9 says, "When I cry unto thee, then shall mine enemies turn back: this I know; for God is for me." The force of depression may not turn back until you lift your voice in desperation to God.

Psalm 61:1-2 says, "1 Hear my cry, O God; attend unto my prayer. 2 From the end of the earth will I cry unto thee, when my heart is overwhelmed: lead me to the rock that is higher than I".

The scripture acknowledges that sometimes our hearts can become overwhelmed, but in the same breath, it offers an antidote - to cry out to God. It further tells us what to cry about—"lead me

---

1.

https://www.healthline.com/health/benefits-of-crying#:~:text=Crying%20may%20support%20both%20the,triggered%20by%20many%20different%20emotions.

to the rock that is higher than I". This suggests crying out to God to lead you into a place of safety in Him, a dimension of serenity and tranquility that only exists in the presence of God.

We have become too self-aware and conscious that we bottle up a lot of negative emotions waiting to explode some day at the slightest triggers. Until we are ready to lose our self-awareness and simply surrender in a desperate cry to God, the enemy will keep oppressing. Everyone reading this book and suffering depression needs to get to where all that matters to you is your wholeness and perfect peace. This is a good point to pause reading and pray this prayer in Isaiah 38:14, NKJV ("Like a crane or a swallow, so I chattered; I mourned like a dove; My eyes fail from looking upward. O Lord, I am oppressed; Undertake for me!").Dear Lord Jesus, I am oppressed and in trouble, please undertake for me. Come to my aid and be my pledge of safety.

Hannah was a woman of many sorrows at a point in her life. I can only imagine the level of depression she had suffered while she waited for her Samuel (1 Samuel 1). Writing this book, I can relate to her struggles, having waited for a while to have a baby. This is a situation you cannot wish for a perceived enemy. For me, it was a monthly torture and distress. Hannah's case was worst because she had Peninnah, her competitor, who made matters worse for her. In 1 Samuel 1:6, the scripture says that, "and her rival also provoked her severely, to make her miserable, because the Lord had closed her womb". Can you imagine living with such a rival, a constant source of pain, provocation, anxiety, and depression? Maybe you have a Peninnah in your life -it could be a person, your past, mistakes, and regrets, constantly staring at you. Look at how Hannah handled her Peninnah.

She offered a vehement cry to God; poured her heart to God in a naked prayer session. She cried out like one who was under an influence. She simply poured out her bitterness to God. What happened next? She got her answer, her tears were wiped away and she became free from her depression. Notice Peninnah was still there, but she no longer had the power over Hannah anymore to determine her mental state and emotions. This is the ultimate victory when the source of depression and pain no longer has power over your life, that equates to dominion. You take away the power of the triggers, and the "chip" that the demon of depression uses to manipulate you with his remote control no longer functions. Just like the psalmist said, He prepares a table before me in the presence of my enemies (Psalm 23:5).

Jesus Christ, in the days of His flesh, when He had offered up prayers and supplications, with vehement cries and tears to Him who was able to save Him from death and was heard because of His godly fear (Hebrews 5:7). Jesus offered His prayers with strong cries and tears, in pain and wept in sorrow to God. This is not about crying out hysterically, but crying out to God for help and deliverance. As I wrap up this chapter, this is one prayer I highly recommend praying as you cry out to God:

Psalm 142:7 "Bring my soul out of prison, That I may praise Your name; The righteous shall surround me, For You shall deal bountifully with me."

Pray this over your soul, your loved ones, friend, sons and daughters, and God will surely hear your cry. Amen.

10

The Spirit of Joy

JOY UNSPEAKABLE, FULL OF GLORY

But the fruit of the [Holy] Spirit [the work which His presence within accomplishes] is love, joy (gladness), peace, patience (an even temper, forbearance), kindness, goodness (benevolence), faithfulness,
Galatians 5:22 (AMPC)

I think it is very important to continue to differentiate between joy and happiness, these two are different. The former is internal, and the latter depends on external triggers. Happiness depends on happenings around your life. It is like a roller coaster. One day you are on top of the mountain because of favorable circumstances and the next day you are down in the valley because of what someone says to you. Joy comes from the Holy Spirit living within a believer. This joy will make you walk in victory, sing and rejoice in the face of contrary situations. We need the type of joy that causes the negative past to lose hold on our present and looks forward with hope into the future.

Joy, for the most part, is not in the events but in the purpose and outcome of the event. Hebrews 12:2 says, "Looking unto Jesus the author and finisher of our faith; who for the joy that was set before him endured the cross, despising the shame, and is set down at the right hand of the throne of God".

The outcome of Jesus's suffering, which is our redemption, stirred up joy within Him in the face of pain. Stop looking for joy in the event, but if you search and set your face on the purpose and outcome of the events, you will find joy even in the most difficult circumstances.

Look at this hymn of faith in Habakkuk 3:17-19, when things don't make sense to you, and everything seems to be falling apart.

Habakkuk 3:17-19 –"17 Although the fig tree shall not blossom, neither shall fruit be in the vines; the labour of the olive shall fail, and the fields shall yield no meat; the flock shall be cut off from the fold, and there shall be no herd in the stalls:

18 Yet I will rejoice in the Lord, I will joy in the God of my salvation.

19 The Lord God is my strength, and he will make my feet like hinds' feet, and he will make me to walk upon mine high places. To the chief singer on my stringed instruments."

Yet in all of these, I will rejoice in the Lord, I will joy in the God of my salvation and not in anything external, connection, or people. I will repose my confidence in God and in His capacity to turn things around. Job said even though He slays me, I will still trust Him (Job 13:15). What a level of faith and trust!

Another important scripture to consider here is Psalm 84:5-6 : "5 Blessed is the man whose strength is in thee; in whose heart are the ways of them. 6 Who passing through the valley of Baca make it a well; the rain also filleth the pools."

The valley of Baca is the valley of weeping, and you are not supposed to pitch your tent there. You are to pass through it and make it a well. Another version says you can pass through the dark valley of tears and dig deep to find a pleasant pool where others find only pain (Psalm 84:5-6, TPT). Others may find pain only, but the Holy Spirit, when engaged can help you dig in the valley to find purpose and a pleasant pool.

Isaiah 61:3, says that God is able to cause an exchange and re-place mourning with the oil of joy. Oil in this context symbolizes the Holy Spirit, which implies He is the original custodian of joy.

We have so much neglected the intrinsic joy that we have within that we have refused to tap into. It is called the joy of the Holy Ghost. Regarding this joy, the Bible states it is an inexpressible and glorious (triumphant, heavenly) joy. Nothing else can match it in this world, no matter the level and degree of entertainment. It is also the fruit of the Spirit. This implies that it is the work which His presence within us accomplishes as we maintain our union with Him. When last did you experience the joy of the Holy Ghost? You can stir up this joy within yourself. Let me mention a few ways to stir up this joy.

Revelation from the word

Jeremiah 15:16 "Thy words were found, and I did eat them; and thy word was unto me the joy and rejoicing of mine heart: for I am called by thy name, O Lord God of hosts."

When you truly find the word with deep insight, it stirs joy automatically and depression cannot stand it. Every time we expose ourselves to God's Word, we are giving our spirits a feast and we get to experience joy inexpressible, full of glory.

This joy comes from what we know. For example, Romans 8:28 says, "And we know that all things work together for good to those who love God, to those who are the called according to His purpose". When you know that God as a Master potter can take even the broken pieces of your life and make a masterpiece out of it, that should stir up joy within you.

Have a song

How do you expect me to have a song in my heart while I am dealing with depression? This sounds unrealistic, right?

The scripture in Isaiah 30:29-30 says,

"29 Ye shall have a song, as in the night when a holy solemnity is kept; and gladness of heart, as when one goeth with a pipe to come into the mountain of the Lord, to the mighty One of Israel.

30 And the Lord shall cause his glorious voice to be heard, and shall shew the lighting down of his arm, with the indignation of his anger, and with the flame of a devouring fire, with scattering, and tempest, and hailstones."

Having a song in your heart is a covenant requirement to ascending to the mountain of the Lord, His Presence, where no depression can coexist with you. Isaiah 54:1 (NKJV) also corroborates this, saying, "Sing, O barren, you who have not borne! Break forth into singing, and cry aloud, you who have not labored with child! For more are the children of the desolate than the children of the married woman," says the Lord. How do you expect a barren woman to sing? This is a scriptural prescription to escape from the hold of depression. You have to sing your way out. Not any song though, but Holy Spirit inspired songs because every song will take you to where it came from. In an empirical study, researchers found a connection between the frequency of listening to religious music and a decrease in death anxiety and increase in life satisfaction, self-esteem, and a sense of control among older U.S. adults[1]

.

Get hold of songs that can lift the soul into the presence of God, where there is liberty of expression for the soul. You can be intentional about it.

Ask the Holy Spirit

1. Bradshaw M, Ellison CG, Fang Q, Mueller C. Listening to Religious Music and Mental Health in Later Life. Gerontologist. 2015 Dec;55(6):961-71. doi: 10.1093/geront/gnu020. Epub 2014 Apr 15. PMID: 24737625.

One effect which the Holy Spirit accomplishes in a yielded believer's life is an intrinsic joy within the heart. This is why joy is a fruit of the Spirit (Galatians 5:22), and that qualifies Him as the custodian of joy. He releases joy within our spirit that gives us stability amid a crisis.

Romans 15:13 encapsulates this very well - "Now the God of hope fill you with all joy and peace in believing, that ye may abound in hope, through the power of the Holy Ghost." He fills us with joy and causes us to abound in hope through the power of the Holy Spirit. Stop looking for joy in the wrong places. The Holy Spirit is the true source of lasting joy that can displace depression. My hope is that you will cry out to God to fill you afresh in increasing dimensions with the Spirit of Joy.

Make this your prayer:

Heavenly Father, in the name of Jesus, I break the hold of the spirit of discouragement and despair over my life. Let your joy, which is full of glory flow out from the depths of my innermost being. I receive the grace by the Holy Spirit to rejoice and praise you in every circumstance in Jesus' name.

11

Shake yourself from the dust

ARISE FROM DEPRESSION

Arise [from the depression and prostration in which circumstances have kept you—rise to a new life]! Shine (be radiant with the glory of the Lord), for your light has come, and the glory of the Lord has risen upon you!
Isaiah 60:1 (AMPC)

One of the marks of biblical faith and covenants is responsibility. There are things that only you can do for yourself. Depending on where you grew up, you may have heard people say in Christian circles, "I am waiting on God". What I have found out many times is that God is waiting on you to take the first step as a proof of your faith in Him. A very respected father of faith,

Bishop David Oyedepo, would say, "every day is God's day but the day your faith comes alive is your day".

Isaiah 60:1 AMPC, says "Arise [from the depression and prostration in which circumstances have kept you—rise to a new life]! Shine (be radiant with the glory of the Lord), for your light has come, and the glory of the Lord has risen upon you!".

It is time to arise from depression into a new life where you begin to exercise your dominion in Christ.

Hannah arose from her depression and her countenance was no longer sad after she encountered God. She went ahead and worshipped God (1 Samuel 1:18-19). Remember she had not had Samuel at this time. But a heart worship becomes your default when you choose to arise because you have had an encounter with God through His word. You burst into worship naturally, without coercion. Saints of God, I say again; it is time to arise.

I love the spiritual postures painted in Isaiah 52:1-2:"1 Awake, awake; put on thy strength, O Zion; put on thy beautiful garments, O Jerusalem, the holy city: for henceforth there shall no more come into thee the uncircumcised and the unclean. 2 Shake thyself from the dust; arise, and sit down, O Jerusalem: loose thyself from the bands of thy neck, O captive daughter of Zion".

This scripture is full of practical instructions that can help to reposition anyone. It says put on your strength, and what is our strength as believers? Nehemiah 8:10 says the joy of the Lord is our strength, not the joy of things or achievements. So we are required to put on our joy, which is our strength. In this context, we can also translate the word strength as stronghold, defense, protection, refuge, fortress, and safety. So, the joy of the Lord is our stronghold, defense, protection, refuge, fortress, and safety. Anything outside of this joy is not safe.

Second, Isaiah 52:1-2 further says, "put on thy beautiful garments" which scripturally refers to our praise (Isaiah 61:3 – "garment of praise instead of a spirit of despair"). So you can wear praise as garment! Look at this beautiful scripture in Psalms 8:2 TPT–"You have built a stronghold by the songs of children. Strength rises up with the chorus of infants. This kind of praise has power to shut Satan's mouth. Childlike worship will silence the madness of those who oppose you".

So, we build strongholds around our emotions with songs, and we rise like an edifice with strength via praise. It ends by saying that there is a kind of praise, childlike worship where you are not bothered by who is in the room. This type of praise can shut Satan's mouth, demonic whisperings trying to pull you into a pit of depression. Saints of God, it is high time we put on our garment of praise! You don't have to wait until you attend a church service. No, you can have a praise break in your room and even within the prison doors because you are about to come out. It's a brand-new day and a new dawn!

Further, Isaiah 52:1-2 gives another instruction–"Shake thyself from the dust" (NIV says "Shake off your dust"). One of the meanings of the word dust is a low condition or the grave. God is commanding you to shake off the dust of fear, anxiety and depression by claiming the promises of God for your life. Break free from every mental chain holding you down and walk in the liberty of the children of God in Christ. When you decide to shake off your dust of the past, you will be amazed to discover that the chains have already been broken and your liberty has already been established.

Rise and sit enthroned is the next instruction. The throne God prepared for you has been vacant for too long. The force of depression has kept you in obscurity for too long. It is time to rise to a new life in Christ Jesus because your light has come, says the Lord (Isaiah 60:1).Do you know that you have been redeemed to reign on the earth? - Romans 5:17 says, "For if by one man's offence death reigned by one; much more they which receive abundance of grace and of the gift of righteousness *shall reign in life* by one, Jesus Christ (italics added)". So, we rise and sit enthroned by grace and righteousness through Jesus the Christ. Our badge of authority in exercising our dominion is on the platform of righteousness (Hebrews 1:8-9).

The last instruction in Isaiah 52:1-2 says "loose thyself from the bands of thy neck". Stop giving room or an opportunity for depression to lay hold on your life. This may imply that you break free from abusive relationships, unplug for a while from the barrage of social media platforms, and so on. Search your life and see things that make you vulnerable. You have the power and unction in Christ to lose yourself from the chains around your neck.

Again, I would like to conclude this book in the words of a great servant of God, Bishop David Oyedepo, "What you don't want, you don't watch; what you don't resist has the right to remain and what you don't confront you cannot conquer". It is time to ARISE in Jesus Name, Amen!.

12

Where the journey to freedom begins from

Be born again. You may have heard this phrase repeatedly, as a church or religious cliché. But this experience births a new nature in you and gives you power over sin, which opens the door to the oppressor. Jesus said to Nicodemus in John 3:3 & 5 (paraphrased), Except a person be born again, one cannot see the kingdom of God and cannot enter the kingdom of God. One cannot experience God or have an intimate experience with Him without surrendering one's life to the Lord Jesus. You may have been in church all your life, but have never asked Jesus to be the Lord and Savior of your life. It is time to do so now.

Say this prayer from your heart:

Heavenly Father, I come to You in the Name of Jesus. I am asking you to come into my heart and be the Lord over my life. I acknowledge that I have sinned against you, but now Lord, have mercy upon me and forgive my sins. Make me clean and whole by the precious blood of Jesus. I confess with my mouth the Lord Jesus and believe in my heart that God has raised him from the dead. I am now born again; I am now a child of God. I am saved in Jesus' name! I now ask you to fill me with Your Holy Spirit to the overflow in Jesus' name, AMEN!

About the author

Dr Michael Emmanuel is a voice that speaks life into the purposes and destinies of men and women. He has a PhD in engineering, and a student of the word of God. He is married to Foluso Emmanuel and they are blessed with 3 adorable children. You can reach him at vintagerevival03@gmail.com

www.ingramcontent.com/pod-product-compliance
Lightning Source LLC
Chambersburg PA
CBHW060349130626
46553CB00003B/1157

* 9 7 9 8 9 9 1 1 9 9 7 0 4 *